Exploring Langu[age]

SERIES EDITOR: RICHARD

Exploring Language

Change

*An anthology of English
from early times to the present day*

MIKE TAYLOR

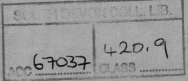

CAMBRIDGE
UNIVERSITY PRESS

Published by the Press Syndicate of the University of Cambridge
The Pitt Building, Trumpington Street, Cambridge CB2 1RP
40 West 20th Street, New York, NY 10011–4211, USA
10 Stamford Road, Oakleigh, Melbourne 3166, Australia

First published 1993

Printed in Great Britain at the University Press, Cambridge

A catalogue record for this book is available from the British Library.

ISBN 0 521 44628 7 paperback

GO

Illustrations on pages 1, 2, 4, 10, 20 and 21 by Sharon Scotland.

Page logo drawn by Amanda MacPhail

Photographs: page 6, Popperfoto; page 8, Imperial War Museum;
page 9, © Grundy, reproduced by permission of BBC Television.

Acknowledgements

Thanks are due to the following for permission to reproduce from copyright material:

page 13, reproduced by kind permission of the Dean and Chapter, Peterborough
Cathedral; page 15, reproduced by permission of the Wellcome Institute Library,
London; pages 17 and 18, reproduced by courtesy of the Essex Record Office,
Chelmsford.

Every effort has been made to reach copyright holders. The publishers would be glad to
hear from anyone whose rights they have unknowingly infringed.

Contents

The anthology of examples in this book has been arranged to illustrate some of the sources you could use to explore how language has changed over the centuries and where modern English has come from.

Reading through the examples, and doing some of the activities suggested in the rest of the book will prepare you for further discoveries and detective work of your own.

Some useful sources for collecting evidence of language change are:

- *documents, memorials and gravestones in and around churches and cathedrals.*
  You may need to ask permission in order to see or photograph some of these.

- *local archives such as historical maps, documents and news-papers. These are usually available in museums and record offices.*

- *books, letters and family heirlooms which your parents or grandparents have collected.*

- *novels, stories, plays and poems written over the past few hundred years or so.*

A Origins of personal names

PEOPLE'S NAMES

Before the eleventh century Anglo-Saxon people had their own single names such as:

Male	Female
Earnwulf	Ethelburga
Cynewulf	Selethrytha
Helmheard	
Heorogar	
Edgar	

The Vikings passed down their personal names to their children, so it became necessary to add descriptive names to identify different children with the same name. For instance, different 'Edgars' might become:

Edgar Shortleg   Edgar Idler   Edgar Drunkard   Edgar Unready

Gradually in Norman times, these additional names became surnames passed on from one generation to another. These could mean 'son (or daughter) of' . . .
For example:

Johnson	Andrews	McDonald	Bevan (ap Evan)
Thomson	Adams	MacRae	Price (ap Rhys)
Harrison	Davies	O'Reilly	Pugh (ap Hugh)

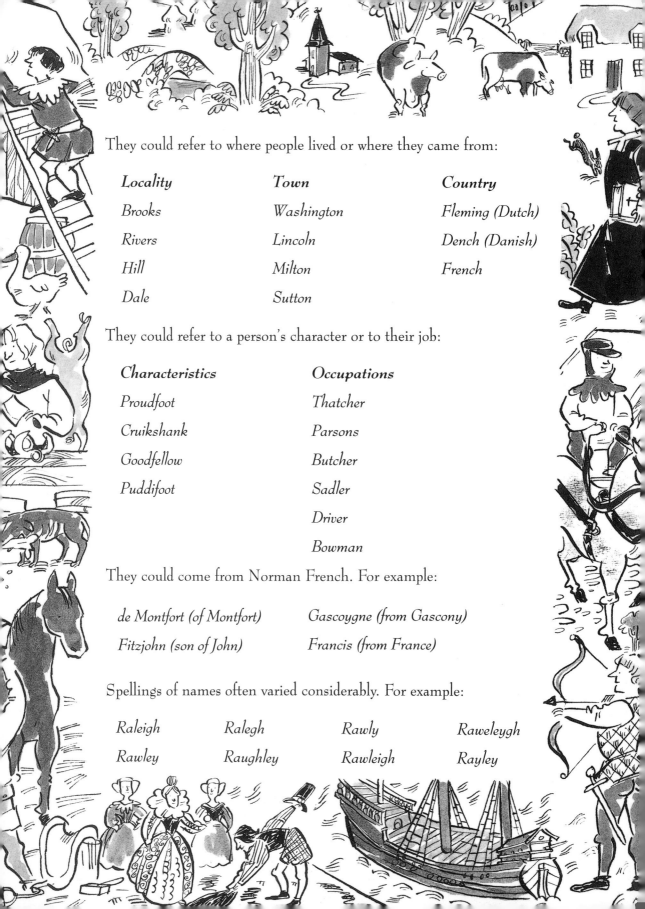

They could refer to where people lived or where they came from:

Locality	Town	Country
Brooks	Washington	Fleming (Dutch)
Rivers	Lincoln	Dench (Danish)
Hill	Milton	French
Dale	Sutton	

They could refer to a person's character or to their job:

Characteristics	Occupations
Proudfoot	Thatcher
Cruikshank	Parsons
Goodfellow	Butcher
Puddifoot	Sadler
	Driver
	Bowman

They could come from Norman French. For example:

de Montfort (of Montfort)   Gascoygne (from Gascony)

Fitzjohn (son of John)   Francis (from France)

Spellings of names often varied considerably. For example:

Raleigh	Ralegh	Rawly	Raweleygh
Rawley	Raughley	Rawleigh	Rayley

B Vicars and prioresses

VICARS OF LEEDS PARISH CHURCH (KENT)

ALEXANDER	1175	JOHN BLACKBURNE	1624
ROBERT	1191	JOHN LOCKWOOD	1625
FOLK	1211	RICHARD MARSH	1635
ROGER	1237	WILLIAM FRANCIS	1641
WILLIAM	1249	NATHANIEL WILLMOT	1643
NICKOLAS	1261	THOMAS PARAMORE	1647
RICHARD	1267	THOMAS CHOWNING	1651
STEPHEN	1283	THOMAS SHEWELL	1659
JOHN	1285	JOHN MOORE	1662
ADAM DE MAYDENSTEN	1299	JAMES WILLSON	1665
WILLIAM DE BORDENNE	1306	EDWARD WATERMAN MA	1685
ADAM	1314	EDWARD HARRISON MA	1725
WILLIAM	1324	DENNY MARTIN FAIRFAX MA	1760
ROBERT DE MAIDSTONE	1347	CHARLES CAGE MA	1794
THOMAS	1368	JAMES YOUNG BA	1795
THOMAS DE ROFFA	1380	WILLIAM HORNE MA	1799
AYMER ODENHELLE	1397	GEORGE ST JOHN MITCHELL	1801
WILLIAM DE VERDUN	1409	THOMAS LOMAS MA	1814
THOMAS OF SIDYNGBOURNE	1409	WILLIAM BURKITT MA	1843
JOHN SURYNDEN	1409	ADOLPHUS PHILIPSE MORRIS MA	1877
JOHN WITTISHAM	1409	HENRY ROBERT HUGHES MA	1906
ROBERT GOUDEHERST	1453	STANLEY NOTHARD SWAIN AKC	1920
JOHN BREDGAR	1487	THOMAS HERBERT JACQUES RA	1927
RICHARD CHETHAM	1495	CYRIL WALLACE CARTER AKC	1936
ARTHUR SENTLEGER	1528	FRED TYRIE AKC	1945
THOMAS DAYE	1536	JOHN ELLIS ROBINSON ALCD	1960
HENRY TILDEN	1557	JOHN WILLIAM DILNOT MA	1974
THOMAS ANGOOD	1610	ADRIAN CHRISTOPHER BELL AKC	1979
WILLIAM CRAGG	1618	CHRISTOPHER MATTISON DENT	1984
MATTHEW LAWRENCE	1622	MA MTh DPhil	

PRIORESSES OF HIGHAM ABBEY (KENT)

Mary, daughter of Stephen	
Juliana	1170
Alice	
Joan de Merliston	1247
Acelina	1266
Amfelisia de Dunlegh	1275
Maud de London	1295
Joan de Handlo	1301
Maud de Grenestede	1329
Elizabeth de Delham	1340
Cecily Leyham	1361
Olive	1388
Joan de Haleghesto	1388
Joan Cobham	1390
Joan Sone	1394
Alice Peacham	1418
Isabel Wade	1419
Margaret Boteler	1462
Christina	1475
Elizabeth Bradforth	1494
Agnes Swayne	1501
Marjory Hilgerden	1509
Anchoreta Ungothorpe	1514

In 1538, when the nuns of Malling Abbey in Kent were pensioned off, sums of money were given to 11 nuns with the following names:

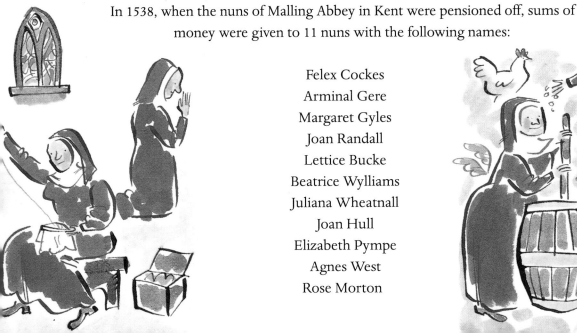

Felex Cockes
Arminal Gere
Margaret Gyles
Joan Randall
Lettice Bucke
Beatrice Wylliams
Juliana Wheatnall
Joan Hull
Elizabeth Pympe
Agnes West
Rose Morton

C Place names

NAMES ADAPTED IN OLD ENGLISH FROM LATIN
For example *ceaster* taken from Latin *castra* (fort)

Cirencester   Lancaster   Chester

SAXON NAMES WITH *-ING* (CHIEFS OF CLANS)

Reading from *Readingas* (Reada's people)
Hastings from *Haestingas* (Haesta's people)

SAXON NAMES WITH *-HAM* (HOMESTEAD)

Egham (Ecga's homestead)   Chobham (Ceabba's homestead)

ALSO   *stowe* (place)   Felixstowe (St Felix's holy place)
       sted (place)   Plumstead (place where plums grow)
tun or *ton* (farm or village)   Brighton (Beorhthelms's farm)

SCANDINAVIAN AND VIKING NAMES

by (farm or village)   Grimsby (Grimr's farm)
wick (dwelling or farm)   Keswick (building [*wic*] where cheese [*cese*] was made)
thorpe (farm or village)   Mablethorpe (Malbert's village)
thwaite (glade or clearing)   Stonethwaite
toft (ground)   Lowestoft (Hloover's plot of ground)

NORMAN NAMES

Beaulieu (beautiful place)
Beaumont (beautiful hill)
Grossmont (large hill)

DID YOU KNOW . . . ?

- Dublin and Blackpool have the same name: *dubh line* means 'black pool'.
- Why in the old county of Yorkshire was there a North Riding, a West Riding and an East Riding but not a South Riding? (Answer: because the county was divided into thirds or *thriddings*.)
- In Celtic *penn* means hill. So when some Celts settled on a large hill in what is now Lancashire, they called it 'Penn'. The Saxons renamed it with their own word *hyll* calling it 'Penn Hyll'. After many years people called it 'Pendle'. Later still the English word *hill* was added. So the place we now call 'Pendle Hill' means 'hill, hill, hill'!
- Over time some Norman names have changed back to English forms. For example: Beaurepaire (beautiful retreat) became Belper, and Chartreuse became Charterhouse.

Basic words

The 100 most common words in English are all Old English, and include: *this, is, you, here, there,* as well as others like *earth, dog, sheep, wood, field, work* and *laughter.*

When Winston Churchill spoke to the British people in 1940 during the darkest days of the Second World War, he used many Old English words:

'We shall fight on the beaches; we
shall fight on the landing grounds;
we shall fight in the fields and in
the streets, we shall fight in the
hills; we will never surrender.'

E Borrowed words

Throughout history, the English language has grown by 'borrowing' words from other countries and their languages. Some of these 'borrowings' were the result of invasions (by the Vikings and the Normans, for example), but most have come into the language through contacts made by travel and trade, or through the reading of classical books written in Latin and Greek. Here are some examples from different stages in history:

ELEVENTH CENTURY

Norman French

tax	judge	soldier	satin	cape	treasurer	jury
robe	battalion	enemy	moat	siege	noble	embroidery

SIXTEENTH AND SEVENTEENTH CENTURIES

Italian

traffic

ducat   ballot

brigand   manage

Latin

genius   appendix

junior   radius

fungus   vacuum

area   species

exit   apparatus

Greek

irony   idea

alphabet   chorus

cosmos   scheme

drama   tonic

rhythm

Spanish

cork   sherry

galleon   cargo

cask   guitar

armada   mosquito

Low German (Dutch)

splint   snort

skipper   easel

yacht   sketch

spool   splice

smuggler   landscape

groove   luck

1940s American and British English

During the Second World War (1939–45), the American War Department issued this list of British English words with their American meanings to help American servicemen and women understand spoken English in Britain.

ad	advert	dessert	sweet course
atomizer	scent spray	junk	rubbish
banked (curve in road)	superelevated	long-distance (telephone call)	trunk
battery	accumulator	peanut	monkey-nut
bingo	housey-housey	porterhouse (steak)	sirloin
bowling alley	skittle alley		
brief case	portfolio	radio	wireless
car (of train) (newspaper)	carriage	raincoat	mackintosh
		scrambled eggs	buttered eggs
clipping	cutting	soft drinks	minerals
commuter		thriller	shocker
cone (ice cream)	season ticket holder cornet	toilet	lavatory

These words and phrases are used by young people in Australia and New Zealand.

Scott Michaelson as Brad Willis from Neighbours © Grundy

chookie	*chicken/hen*
sprigs	*boot studs*
lollies	*sweets*
sand-shoes	*plimsolls, canvas shoes*
jug	*electric kettle*
dairy	*corner shop which is open all hours and sells everything*
to spragg	*to thwart*
tramping	*hiking*
she's right mate	*everything is fine*
what's the story?	*what's it all about?*
to feel crook	*to feel unwell*
to be tinny	*to be lucky*
a joker	*a man*
a piker	*someone who backs out of an agreement*
goodday	*hello*

F Lost words

As well as gaining new words by 'borrowing' words from other languages, language changes as words fall from use. Here are some words from 1370 which are no longer used:

alose	*praise*
awhape	*amaze*
baude	*lively*
beme	*trumpet*
bretful	*brimful*
chalon	*blanket*
cheeste	*quarrelling*
clapers	*rabbit holes*
cuer	*heart*
decoped	*slashed*
drasty	*filthy*
drovy	*muddy*
grodde	*rub*
gyte	*dress*
jilbke	*jug*
mappemounde	*map of the world*
wlonk	*proud*
wonger	*pillow*

ST MATTHEW'S GOSPEL, CHAPTER 17

Version 1: Modern English
The Jerusalem Bible (1966)

Six days later, Jesus took with him Peter and James and his brother John and led them up a high mountain where they could be alone. There in their presence he was transfigured: his face shone like the sun and his clothes became as white as the light. Suddenly Moses and Elijah appeared to them; they were talking with him. Then Peter spoke to Jesus. 'Lord,' he said, 'it is wonderful for us to be here';

Version 2: Early Modern English
The Authorised Version (1611)

And after six days Jesus taketh Peter, James, and John his brother, and bringeth them up into an high mountain apart, and was transfigured before them: and his face did shine as the sun, and his raiment was white as the light. And, behold, there appeared unto them Moses and Elias talking with him. Then answered Peter, and said unto Jesus, Lord, it is good for us to be here:

Version 3: Middle English
The Wycliffe Bible (1382)

And after sexe dayes Jhesus toke Petre, and Jamys, and Joon, his brother, and ledde hem asydis in to an hiʒ hill, and was transfigured bifore hem. And his face schoon as the sunne; forsothe his clothis were maad white as snow. And lo ! Moyses and Helye apperiden to hem, spekynge with hym. Sothely Petre answerynge seid to Jhesu, Lord, it is good vs to be here.

Version 4: Old English
The West Saxon Gospels (AD 1000)

And æfter six dagum nam[1] se Hǣlend[2] Petrum, and Iacobum, and Iohannem, hys brōor, and lǣdde hig on-sundron[3] on ǣnne heahne munt,[4] and he wæs gehīwod[5] beforan him. And his ansȳn[6] sceān swā swā[7] sunne; and hys reaf[8] wǣron swā hwīte swā snāw. And efne[9]! ā[10] ætȳwde[11] Moyses and Helias, mid[12] him sprecende. Đā cwþ [13] Petrus to him, Drihten,[14] gōd ys ūs hēr tō bēonne.

[1]took [2]the Lord [3]together [4]mountain [5]transfigured [6]countenance [7]as [8]garments [9]lo, behold [10]then [11]appeared [12]with [13]said [14]Lord

In 1066, the Normans conquered England. For many years Norman French was the official language used for law, administration, and writing literature. Ordinary people, however, continued to speak Old English. Over time, many educated Saxon and Norman people learned both languages. The languages began to merge, although English regained the upper hand. This new English is called Middle English.

The Canterbury Tales by Geoffrey Chaucer is the most famous book written in Middle English. It is a series of poems about a group of pilgrims travelling from London to the shrine of Thomas Becket at Canterbury. On the way, each pilgrim tells a story. This is the description of the young Squire who is travelling with his father, the Knight.

	With him ther was his sone, a yong SQUYER,
	A lovyere, and a lusty bacheler,
crulle *curly*	With lokkes crulle, as they were leyd in presse.
	Of twenty yeer of age he was, I gesse.
	Of his stature he was of evene lengthe,
	And wonderly deliver, and greet of strengthe.
chivachye *cavalry*	And he had been somtyme in chivachye,
	In Flaundres, in Artoys and Picardye,
	And born him wel, as of so litel space,
	In hope to stonden in his lady grace.
Embrouded *embroidered*	Embrouded was he, as it were a mede
	Al ful of fresshe floures, whyte and rede.
floytinge *playing the flute*	Singinge he was, or floytinge, al the day;
	He was as fresh as is the month of May.
	Short was his goune, with sleves longe and wyde.
	Wel coude he sitte on hors, and faire ryde.
endyte *write*	He coude songes make and wel endyte,
Juste *joust* purtreye *draw*	Juste and eke daunce, and wel purtreye and wryte.
	So hote he lovede, that by nightertale
	He sleep namore than dooth a nightingale.
Curteys *courteous, polite*	Curteys he was, lowly, and servisable,
carf *carved*	And carf biforn his fader at the table.

Old Scarlett

YOV SEE OLD SCARLETTS PICTVRE
STAND ON HIE

BVT AT YOVR FEETE HERE DOTH
HIS BODY LYE

HIS GRAVESTONE DOTH HIS AGE
AND DEAH TIME SHOW

HIS OFFICE BY HEIS TOKENS
YOV MAY KNOW

SECOND TO NONE FOR STRENGH
AND STVRDYE LIMM

A SCAREBABE MIGHTY VOICE
WITH VISAGE GRIM

HEE HAD INTERD TWO QVEENES
WITHN HIS PLACE

AND HIS TOWNES HOVSE HOLDERS
IN HIS LIVES SPACE.

TWICE OVER: BVT AT LENGH HIS
OWN TVRN CAME

WHAT HE FOR OTHERS DID FOR
HIM THE SAME

WAS DONE: NO DOVBT HIS SOVLE
DOH LIVE FOR AYE

IN HEAVEN: THO HERE HIS BODY
CLAD IN CLAY

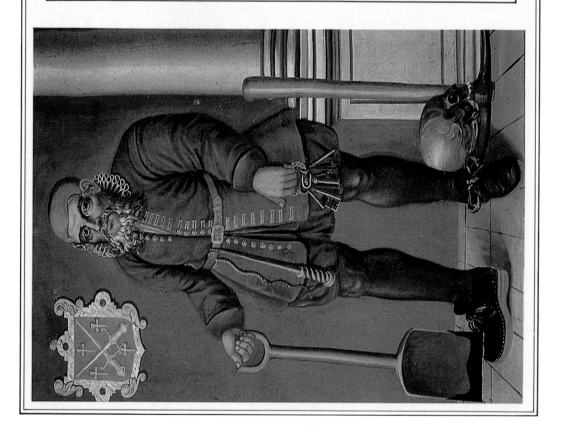

SACRED *to the Memory of*
JOHN POCOCK TINDAL
late of this Parifh
(fecond Son of ROBERT TINDAL & SALLY his wife)
Who in the 17th Year of his Age
was killed in the Moment of Victory
by a Cannon Shot in the memorable Engagement
between the Enlifh & Dutch Fleets
on the 11th October 1797
whilft gallantly on Duty as Signal Midfhipman
on board his Majesty's Ship MONARCH

For his ingenuous and unaffected Manners
his unblemifh'd Integrity & Rectitude of Conduct
he was endeared to many Friends
by whom he has fallen forely and fincerely lamented
To his afflicted Parents & Family he has
left the only Confolation
fo fatal a Cataftrophe can admit
in the Hope
that his truly Chriftian-like Conduct
will thro' Faith *in the Merits of his SAVIOUR*
be assessed and rewarded by his CREATOR
and on the Reflection
that his Life tho' fhort was
virtuous and meritorious
his Death glorious and honourable

The Difeafes and Cafualties this Week.

Abortive	6	Kingfevil	10
Aged	54	Lethargy	1
Apoplexie	1	Murthered at Stepney	1
Bedridden	1	Palfie	2
Cancer	2	Plague	3880
Childbed	23	Plurifie	1
Chrifomes	15	Quinfie	6
Collick	1	Rickets	23
Confumption	174	Rifing of the Lights	19
Convulfion	88	Rupture	2
Dropfie	40	Sciatica	1
Drownd two, one at St.Kath. Tower, and one at Lambeth	2	Scowring	13
Feaver	353	Scurvy	1
Fiftula	1	Sore legge	1
Flox and Small-pox	10	Spotted Feaver and Purples	190
Flux	2	Starved at Nurfe	1
Found dead in the Street at St.Bartholomew the Lefs	1	Stilborn	8
Frighted	1	Stone	2
Gangrene	1	Stopping of the ftomach	16
Gowt	1	Strangury	1
Grief	1	Suddenly	1
Griping in the Guts	74	Surfeit	87
Jaundies	3	Teeth	113
Impofthume	18	Thrush	3
Infants	21	Tiffick	6
Killed by a fall down ftairs at St. Thomas Apoftle	1	Ulcer	2
		Vomiting	7
		Winde	8
		Wormes	18

Chriftned { Males 83, Females 83, In all 166 } Buried { Males 2656, Females 2663, In all 5319 } Plague 3880

Increafed in the Burials this Week —— 1289
Parifhes clear of the Plague —— 34 Parifhes Infected —— 96

London July the 18 1665

Honoured Sir

Blessed be the lord I got to London safe on Wensday by eleven of
the clock and there is but very little notice tooke of the sicknesse here
in London though the bills are very great. There dyd threescore
and 18 in St Giles in the feild scince the bill, and 5 in one hour in our
parish scince. It spreads very much. I went by many houses
in London that were shut up - all over the city almost. Nobody that
is in London feares to goe anywhere but in St Giles's. They
have a bellman there with a cart. There dye so many that
the bell would hardly ever leave ringing and so they ring
not at all. The citizens begin to shut up apace; nothing
hinders them from it but fear of the houses breaking open.
My fathers has beene shut up about a weeke, but theyr is
hardly an house open in the Strand, nor the Exchange. The sicknesse
is at Tottenham high crosse but Mr. Moyse would not have
you let his son know. It is much at Hogsden, so that I saw
them as I went in the road ly in a small thackt house, and I
believe all most starved so great a dread it strikes into the
people. I tarryd in London till Thursday in the afternoon because
the tide would not serve, but then went to Windsor. I have not
as yet been with my father but when I have he will see
how he shall returne you that mony. Sir if you please you may
direct your letter to one Mr Leman next doore to our
house and he will send it us. It is very credibly reported that De
Ryter is beat and taken or sunke. One Wensday night such
news came from Hampton Court. The sicknesse is at Richmond and
we beleeve the king will reside not there long.

Thus with my humble service to you and Mr Blith Junior
I rest your obedient pupill
Samuel Herne

Trade names

When manufacturers create names for their products, the names can rapidly become part of everyday use. The trade or brand names often become so common that we use them rather than the actual name of the appliance. For example, we 'hoover' the carpet even when we are using an Electrolux.

Here are some other trade names which have been adopted into everyday language:

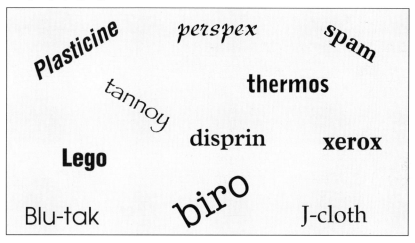

Manufacturers and advertisers will often use 'wrong' spellings to catch our eye and to register their copyright. Here are some examples:

These are 'male' and 'female' versions of similar words. Originally they both shared the same meaning, for instance a brewster was a female brewer. Over the years, however, these meanings have changed.

carlman	wifman
brewer	brewster
baker	baxter
patron	matron
master	mistress
host	hostess
waiter	waitress
Lord	Lady
actor	actress
landlord	landlady
bachelor	spinster
wizard	witch
gentleman	gentlewoman
duke	duchess
governor	governess
dog	bitch
fox	vixen

In the eighteenth century, Dr Samuel Johnson, the lexicographer, and some of his contemporaries strongly disapproved of these words because they were too 'low':

In the nineteenth century, a vicar called Reverend Mursell was disgusted by the use of the following slang expressions:

walks his chalks, cuts his sticks, bolts, cuts his lucky, makes tracks, slopes (all mean 'to go away')

spout (speak)
shut up (stop talking)
hard up (short of money)
the Rhino, the needful, tin, the ready (all mean 'money')

What to look for

Over the centuries, changes in language have taken place in a number of ways. You may find the following ideas helpful when you are discussing the examples in this book, or examples of language change which you have found elsewhere.

Words and meanings

New words have entered the language; some may have been 'invented', some borrowed from other languages. Many words have changed their meaning. Many words have fallen out of everyday use, or have been 'lost' altogether.

Grammar

There have been no major changes in English grammar since around the fourteenth century. Before this time there were differences in word order and word endings. In fact, the grammar of Old English was more like Latin, German or Russian, using the endings of words (or 'cases'), to express relationships between them. The words used to link sentences together were also different in Old English and have changed over the years.

Spelling

Many words have changed their spellings over the years. Spelling was not standardised until the eighteenth century, and many variations were in use (sometimes within the same document!).

Layout, printing and handwriting

There have been different fashions and influences on the way in which information has been set down. For example, the influence of classical learning in the sixteenth to eighteenth centuries led to distinctive 'Roman' styles in lettering and printing. The Victorians, on the other hand, preferred elaborate and florid lettering.

How language grows and changes

Language is likely to go on changing in the future. Here are a few suggestions as to how language has changed, and how it may continue to do so.

By clipping (shortening) words
lab   pub   exam   gym   memo   phone   zoo

By blending two or more words
chortle   smog   brunch

By linking two or more words
after-sales   convenience food   motorway   story-line
credit squeeze

By borrowing words or parts of words from Latin or Greek
(these are often used to create new scientific words)

de-   mono-   epi-   hypo-   neo-   infra-   meta-
micro-   -scope   -ology

By repetition
chit-chat   clip-clop   criss-cross   fuddy-duddy

By creating words from initials
NATO   radar   scuba   NASA   FIAT

By inventing totally new words
Kodak (1888)   PC
rayon (1924)   narrowcast

By extending specialist scientific and technological words into everyday use
interface   software   high tech   on-line

By turning nouns into verbs (or vice versa)
'You bus; I'll foot it into town.'
'This mistake will dog you throughout your career.'
'He womanised while he stayed at the hotel.'

How meanings change

Look at the following examples:

Words can extend their meaning
In Middle English virtue was a male quality. Today it applies to both sexes.

Words can narrow their meaning

In sixteenth-century English mete *(meat) referred to food in general. Today it applies to only one kind.*

Words can shift their meaning

Navigator *once applied only to ships. Now we can use it for road and air travel. The word* crane, *meaning a bird with a long neck, is now also used for a machine to lift things. The word* shrimp, *a small creature, can now mean anyone who is small in stature.*

Words can lose 'bad' meanings

Mischievous *originally meant 'disastrous'.*

Words can gain 'bad' meanings

Notorious *once meant 'very well-known'. Now it means 'strongly disapproved of'.*

Activities to focus on specific examples

A Origins of personal names

Many of our surnames carry with them a long history of meanings which go back over many centuries. Some surnames have remained largely unchanged for hundreds of years. Others have altered in various ways, including changes in:

- spelling. For example, *Browne/Brown*; *Deadman*, which comes from *Debenham* in Suffolk.

- meaning. *Moody* meant 'courageous'; *Pratt* meant 'a cunning man'.

- use. *Stringer* meant 'a person who strings bows'.

Names also reflect the changes and differences in English brought about by factors such as:

- the Norman invasion of 1066.

- the differences in spelling in handwritten and printed English which remained until both printing and the writing of dictionaries became widespread. These differences also remind us of how many different varieties of spoken English (regional dialects) there were at the time.

- the 'classical' (Latin and Greek) influences of eighteenth-century scholars.

ACTIVITY 1

- Looking at the list of surnames, are there any names you recognise?

- Many of the names listed are men's names. Why do you think it is harder to find authentic women's names from this period?

- Many British surnames derive from different words meaning 'son of'. Are all naming systems male-dominated? Are there any countries where children take their mother's name?

EXPLORATION

Make a copy of your class register. Use the names to make the following survey:

For English names

Use the following categories to describe how people may originally have got their surnames:

son of . . .   where they lived . . .   characteristics . . .   job or occupation. . . .

Fit as many surnames as you can into these categories. You will have to do quite a lot of guessing!

Which types of name are most common?

For names from other countries and languages

Find out the literal meaning of the name if you can (see if its owner knows!). Find out whether the names started in a similar way to English names, or whether they work on a different principle.

ACTIVITY 2

You could rename the members of your class using similar categories to decide new names for them. Naming by 'characteristics' should cause some amusement, but make sure that none of your names are rude or offensive.

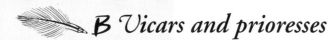

B Vicars and prioresses

Churches are living museums of language and changes in language over time. A local church, particularly an old one, is an ideal place for some detective work into language change. Lists of priests and vicars, gravestones and memorials, bibles and church records all contain evidence of where Modern English has come from, and how language has changed over hundreds of years.

ACTIVITY 1

Look at the names taken from lists of priests and prioresses. Find at least one name which could fit each of the categories listed in the class register activity from Section A.

ACTIVITY 2

- Find some examples from the lists of names which are similar to names used today, but which are spelt differently. Can you see any patterns in the way in which the spelling has changed?

- Find examples of first names which are no longer used today. Where names are unfamiliar, invent a theory about their possible origin.

EXPLORATION

Visit some churches in your own area, and collect examples of names from the parish registers (in which births, marriages and deaths are recorded). You could check the origin of the names using a reference book like *The Guinness Book of Names*, which contains many details about the origin of different surnames.

C *Place names*

The names of places also tell us a lot about the ways in which history has influenced the English language.

EXPLORATION

- Look at a map of your local area or the county in which you live. Find any place names which could be Anglo-Saxon, Viking, or Norman.

- Use a dictionary of place names to check whether your guesses are correct.

- If you can get hold of some old maps of the same area, see if any names have changed over the past 500 years, and note any changes in spelling.

- Look at a map of England. In which parts of England do you find place names ending in:

  -wich
  -ham
  -by
  -caster?

NEW NAMES

Do some research in your local area. What kind of names are given to new roads or new buildings? If you know of any new towns built during the past 50 years, find out how they got their names.

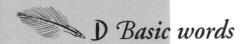

D Basic words

While English has grown and changed over the past 1,000 years, its basic building blocks – the 100 most common words – have remained much the same as they were in Anglo-Saxon times.

EXPLORATION
Find out what some of the 100 most common words in English are. You could do this in a number of ways:

• Look at your own writing, or any written text, and note the most frequently used words.

• Look through some reading books for young children. These often use basic words in the early stages.

• Look at a beginner's book for learning English as a second language.

ACTIVITY 1
In the short extract from Churchill's famous speech, only one word does not come from Old English. Which word do you think it is?

What reasons do you think Churchill might have had for using this simple, Old English vocabulary?

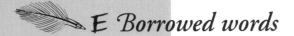

E Borrowed words

One of the ways in which English has changed over the centuries is through the addition of new words. Many of these have been 'borrowed' from other languages.

ACTIVITY 1
Look through the list which gives examples of some borrowed words (there are, of course, many hundreds more than this). Then copy out the grid below and put some of the borrowed words into the different categories.

Fortification, armies, weapons . . .
Food and drink . . .
The arts . . .
Ships and navigation . . .
Science . . .
Politics and the law . . .
Clothes . . .

EXPLORATION

English has continued to 'borrow' words right up to the present day. Make a list of words which we use now which have been borrowed more recently from countries such as Russia, Japan, Australia and America.

Do you know of any other countries which have contributed words to the English language recently?

1940s American and British English

ACTIVITY 2

Which do you think is the American and which the British English list? What has happened to these words since 1940? Would this list be of any use to an American visitor today?

EXPLORATION

Talk about some of the reasons why American English words have now become part of our everyday language. Using any knowledge you may have about America and American English, make a list of some more words which we now use which originally came from the USA.

Australian and New Zealand words

EXPLORATION

With the popularity of television programmes from 'Down Under' it is likely that 'Australian' English will become more widely used in Britain. Do a survey of Australian soap programmes, and while you are watching, note down any words or phrases which are not (as yet) widely used in British English. See how familiar your friends are with the meanings of these words.

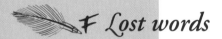

F Lost words

As new words are gained, some are lost.

EXPLORATION

Interview older people who can remember life during or before the Second World War. Ask them if they can think of some words they used when they were young which are not in common use now. Some might be local (dialect) words or slang words.

Sometimes your parents might use slang words which you would never use (for instance to express approval/disapproval). Make a list of these and compare them with lists from other members in your class.

ACTIVITY 1
Using the list of 'lost' words which were in use in 1370, write a short story or 'mini-saga'. Use as many of the words as you can.

6 Different versions of the Bible

These are four versions of the same extract from St Matthew's gospel, Chapter 17, in the New Testament (the story of Jesus).

The versions come from Bibles printed in 1000, 1382, 1611 and 1966.

ACTIVITY 1
- With a friend, read aloud the most recent version (Version 1).

- Now look at Version 2.

- Note down some of the words which are different from those in Version 1. Copy out and complete the chart below, following the example given.

Version 1	Version 2	Version 3	Version 4
led	bringeth		

- Now do the same again, this time comparing Version 2 with Version 3. Fill in the words on your chart under the appropriate headings.

- Now that you are familiar with the meaning of the extract, you can have a go at Version 4, which is written in Old English. Try to work out as much as you can with a friend. Add the words to the chart, as before.

- If you can get hold of bibles written in Danish or German, compare the same passage in these languages with the Old English version. Are there any similarities?

ACTIVITY 2

From the detective work you have done, you will have found some clues about the ways in which English has changed between 1000 and the present day. Make some notes on your discoveries, looking especially at:

- spellings

- the order of words in sentences

- word endings which signal plurals

- word endings which signal tenses, e.g. present and past

- the way the alphabet was printed or handwritten.

EXPLORATION

There are several modern day translations and versions of the Bible. Compare the ways in which they deal with this particular extract from St Matthew's gospel. Which do you prefer?

 **H** *The Canterbury Tales*

ACTIVITY 1

Working with a friend, try reading the description of the squire aloud. Don't worry if you do not know how to say some of the words – have a guess!

ACTIVITY 2

Now write down in Modern English some of the things that Chaucer tells us about the squire. Try to find out:

- what his hairstyle was like

- how old he was

- where he had fought with the army

- what he was wearing

- what skills he had.

Old Scarlett

ACTIVITY 1
Read aloud this epitaph for a gravedigger which was painted on the wall of Peterborough Cathedral in the mid-sixteenth century. Working with the help of a friend, try to guess the meanings of the unfamiliar words.

ACTIVITY 2
Note down some of the differences between the English used here and Modern English.
   Look at:

- letters of the alphabet which are used differently

- words you recognise which are written differently

- words which are familiar to you, but which have changed their meaning since this epitaph was written

- unfamiliar words which you do not understand.

John Pocock Tindal

ACTIVITY 3
Read aloud this epitaph for a young man killed in battle. It is from a monument in Chelmsford Cathedral. Work out how to say some of the words with the help of a friend.

ACTIVITY 4
Many of the words here are still used in formal written English, but they are unlikely to be in everyday use. Using a dictionary, look up the words that you don't know and write the meanings down.

ACTIVITY 5
Rewrite the second part of this epitaph using simpler words. When you have finished, read your version and then the original version aloud. Do the new words make a difference? Do you prefer your own version or the original?

ACTIVITY 6

The mason who carved the stone of this memorial has been very careful in the way he has used capital letters. They are not always used in the way we might expect. Work out a theory to explain the reasons why certain words start with or are written entirely in capitals.

EXPLORATION

Imagine you have been asked to write an epitaph for a 17-year-old killed in the Falklands or the Gulf War. Try to make it sincere and solemn, but without sounding too pompous.

The Great Plague of London

These two documents come from the time of the London plague of 1665.

The first is an early example of statistical information. It is a document of the time listing the different causes of death during one week.

The second is a letter written by Samuel Herne to a Mr Blith. It describes Herne's visit to London, the spread of the plague and the action people were taking to avoid it. Mention is also made of the naval war with the Dutch which was going on at the time.

ACTIVITY 1

Look at the list of diseases and casualties. Copy out the grid below, and divide the list into different causes of death:

Diseases	Accidents or violent death	Not sure

Pick out examples of the following:

- words which have the same meaning as today and the same spelling as today

- words which have the same meaning as today, but are spelled differently

- words which are no longer used. You could check these by looking to see if they are, or are not, in the dictionary.

ACTIVITY 2

Working with a partner, try reading Samuel Herne's letter aloud.

Rewrite the letter in Modern English, noting down where and how spellings have changed since the seventeenth century. (If you divide up the work between several class members, you can write a combined 'translation' and compare notes on the changes in spelling.)

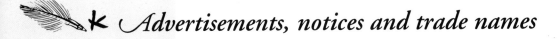

Advertisements, notices and trade names

Wesleyan Day School advertisement (1843)

ACTIVITY 1

Read through the advertisement. Note down any words which you don't understand, or which may have changed their meaning. Guess what they might mean, and then find out the real meaning using a dictionary.

ACTIVITY 2

- How has the lettering in the advertisement been used to support the information being given?

- Is the printer's choice of lettering random, or can you see reasons for particular choices?

ACTIVITY 3

Create an advertisement using a similar style of language which describes your own school or class. Either use different styles of handwriting to highlight particular parts of your advertisement, or experiment with different fonts on a word-processor.

Reward notice

ACTIVITY 4

Choose a crime story from your local paper and write your own reward notice. Try to imitate the nineteenth-century style of language used in the 'Seven Pounds Reward' notice.

Are there any documents in your house which are written in language like this? Ask the adults in your house if you can look at any legal documents such as deeds, wills and insurance policies. Why do you think the language used in such documents is old-fashioned?

Trade names

Collect as many examples as you can of trade names which have now become more generally used.

Collect as many examples as you can to show how manufacturers or advertisers have deliberately used 'wrong' spellings to identify or sell a product. Try looking at advertisements in magazines, trade directories or telephone books and advertisements on television or on hoardings.

Working in small groups, discuss and debate:

- some positive reasons why advertisers use deliberate mis-spellings

- some reasons why people might disapprove.

Language and gender

One of the positive changes which has taken place in English over the past 20 years is the attempt by writers, editors, and publishers to stop language being sexist. However, plenty of examples still slip through, and many older books will contain English that appears to discriminate against women.

- Look through as many older books as you can find at home or in the school library.

- Are there any examples of 'sexist' language?

- When people in general are being referred to, which pronouns are used: 'he', 'she', or 'they'?

- Is 'man' used in encyclopaedias or reference books to mean 'people', or 'the human race'?

ACTIVITY 1

- Look at the list of 'male' and 'female' versions of similar words. They are all examples of language change which relate to gender. Most of them have changed in meaning or fallen from use over the centuries.

- Make a table using the following headings:

  This pair of words is no longer in use.
  Both words (male or female) still have similar meanings.
  The male term has gained a more positive meaning.
  The female term has gained a more negative meaning.

Look at each pair of words in the list and decide where they fit into your table.

- Compare your version of the table with those of other members of the class. Talk together about your findings.

ACTIVITY 2

Invent some sentences, or improvise a dialogue, using each of the terms in the list. Then ask other class members to decide whether the two words share similar meanings or not.

# *Bad language – now and then*

EXPLORATION

- Look at the words and phrases which were considered 'bad language' in previous centuries.

- Are there any other words and phrases which are acceptable today which your grandparents or their parents might have frowned upon? Interview an older person and ask them.